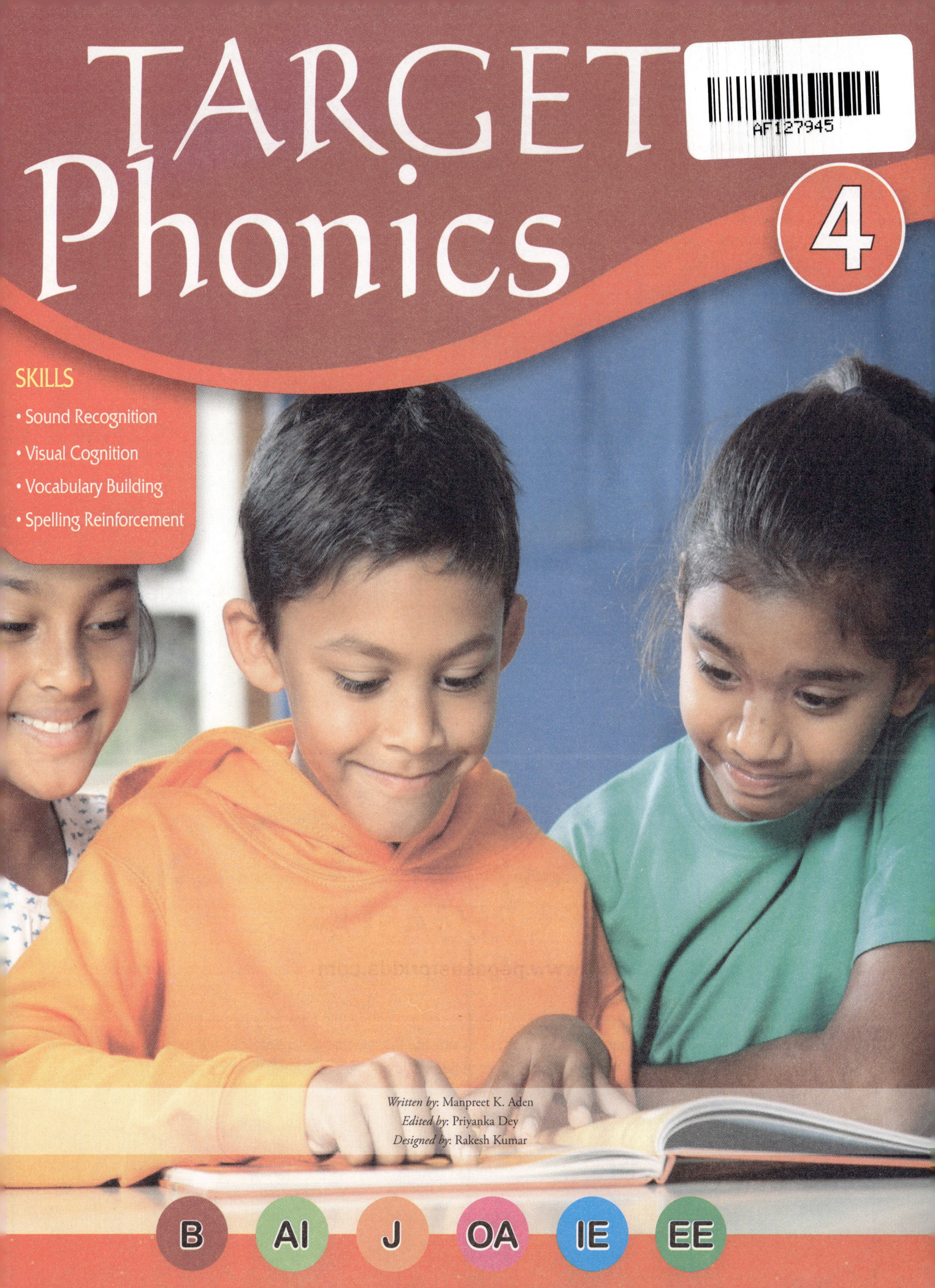

www.pegasusforkids.com

© B. Jain Publishers (P) Ltd. All rights reserved. No part of this book may be reproduced, stored in a retrieval system or transmitted, in any form or by any means, mechanical, photocopying, recording or otherwise, without any prior written permission of the publisher.

Published by Kuldeep Jain for B. JAIN PUBLISHERS (P) Ltd., D-157, Sector 63, Noida - 201307, U.P

Printed in India

B sound

Binny the beaver rolled a barrel of berries to his home.

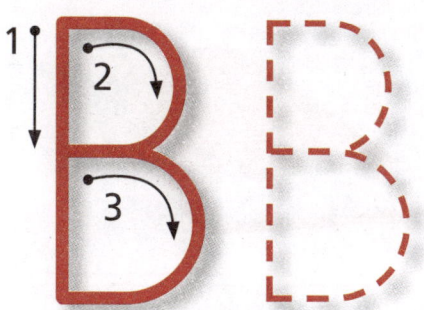

Write the B sound.

B sound words

Basket

Book

Boat

Barrel

Bubble

Belt

Activity

Pair the sounds.

Match the given pictures with their names.

(bagpipe image)	Bamboo
(broom image)	Badge
(beads image)	Broom
(badge/shield image)	Bread
(bread image)	Beads
(bamboo image)	Bagpipe

5

Activity
What's the sound?

Identify all the pictures and write the names of those that begin with the sound B.

AI sound

The sailor was afraid to see a snail in his sailboat.

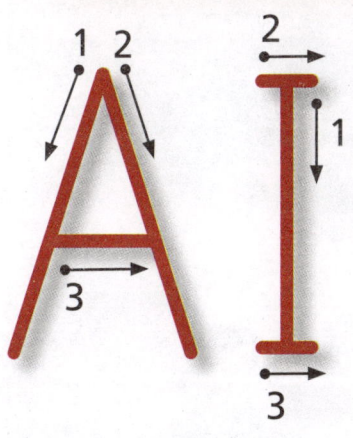

Write the AI sound.

AI

AI sound words

Rain

Tailor

Nail

Train

Chair

Mermaid

Activity

What's the name?

Look at the pictures given below. Write their names in the space provided.

9

Activity
Rhyming words.

Read the words given below. Then think of one word that rhymes with each of these words and write it in the space provided. Remember, all the words you think of must have the AI sound.

Mail

Grain

Hair

Hail

Quail

Air

J sound

Joey the jaguar jumped with joy when he won a jeep.

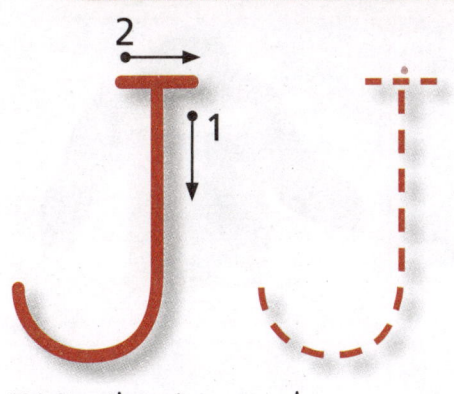

Write the J sound.

J sound words

Jewels

Jackal

Juice

Jet

Joker

Jacket

Activity

Missing sounds.

Look at the pictures given below and write the missing sounds of the given words.

___uggle

___eep

___elly

___ail

___ungle

___udge

Activity

Colour the J sound.

Look at the pictures given below. Read aloud their names and colour the ones that begin with the J sound.

Jam	Juice
Shoe	Judo
Chair	Jeep
Jug	Fan

OA sound

The goat went up the broad moat looking for her missing coat.

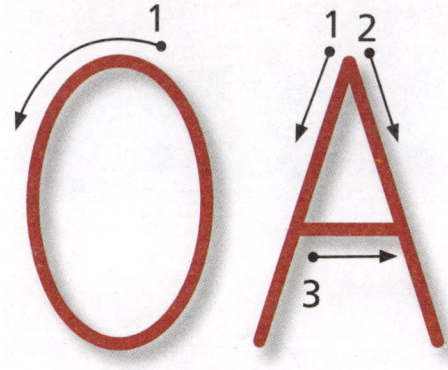

Write the OA sound.

OA

OA sound words

Float

Goat

Coach

Coast

Toast

Cockroach

Activity

Rhyme word pairs.

Read aloud all the words given below in the box. Then place words that rhyme with each other in the space provided.

> Cloak, Coast, Oar, Toad, Coal, Broach, Moat, Float
> Goat, Road, Toast, Oak, Bloat, Boar, Goal, Coach

1.
2.
3.
4.
5.
6.
7.
8.

Activity

The sound web.

Write all the words that have the same OA sound as in Coat.

IE sound

Charlie tried to wear his tie as he ate his pie.

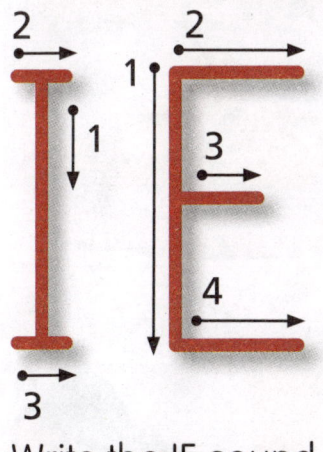

Write the IE sound.

Ie

IE sound words

Chillies

Fries

Coolie

Pie

Priest

Thief

Activity

Identify the IE sound.

How many objects given below have the IE sound in them? Write their names in the space provided.

Shield	 Flies
 Magpie	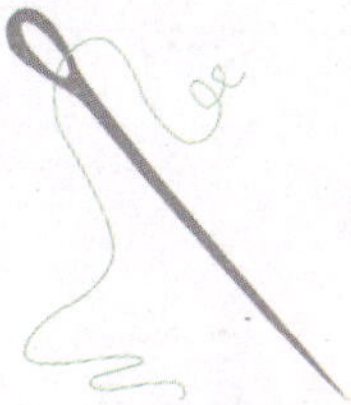 Needle
 Book	 Tie
 Field	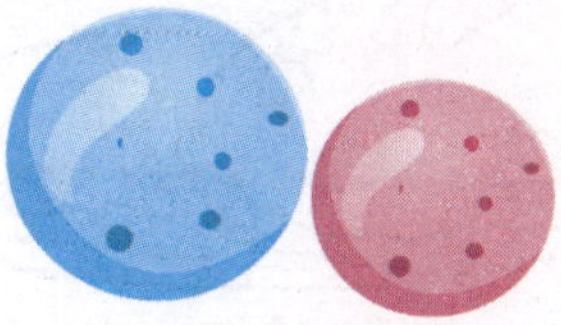 Marble

Activity

Colour the IE sound.

Look at the pictures given below. Colour the ones that have the IE sound as in Piece. Also write their names.

22

EE sound

The queen bee braved the breeze to greet her fleet of bees.

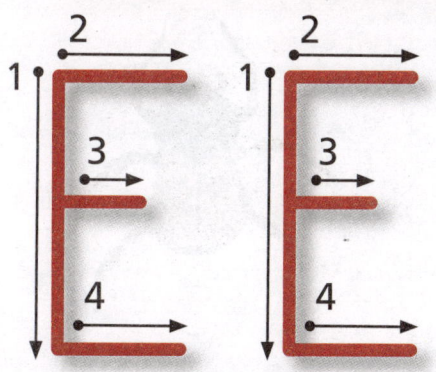

Write the EE sound.

EE sound words

  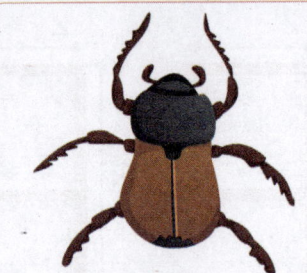

  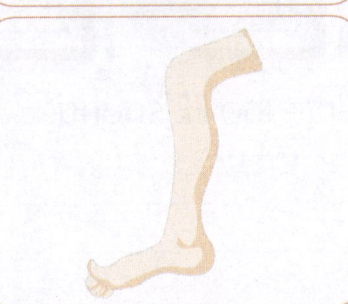

See-saw

Sheep

Street

Beetle

Knee

Seaweed

Activity

Rhyming words.

Read the words given below. Then think of one word that rhymes with each of these words and write it in the space provided. Remember, all the words you think of must have the EE sound.

See

Three

Freeze

Sheep

Street

Heel

Activity

Pair the sounds.

Look at the pictures given below. Match them with their names. Also, write 5 words that have the EE sound in them. Say these words aloud.

(fan)	Face
(feet)	Forest
(forest)	Fountain
(fountain)	Faucet
(faucet)	Feet
(face)	Fan

Let's Practice

Pair rhyming words.

Read aloud all the words given below in the box. Then place the words that rhyme with each other in the space provided.

> Fries, Mountain, Brain, Pain, Thief, Shield, Sail, Pie
> Tail, Rain, Train, Fountain, Tie, Chief, Cries, Field

1.
2.
3.
4.
5.
6.
7.
8.

Let's Practice

Rewind.

Look at the sounds written in the three boxes below. Write at least 5 words that have each of these sounds.

| AI | OA | IE |

Let's Practice

Colour the sounds B, J.

Look at the objects given below and colour the ones that begin with the sounds B and J.

Let's Practice

Pair the sounds.

Look at the pictures given below. Match them with their names that have the sounds OA and EE.

(cheese)	Sleep
(cheetah)	Koala
(cockroach)	Toast
(sleep)	Cheese
(toast)	Cockroach
(koala)	Cheetah
16	Sixteen
(oak tree)	Oak

Let's Practice

Catch the EE and B words.

Read the words given in the cloud. Now find the names of all those pictures from the cloud that have the sounds EE and B in them and write them in the given space.

Bundle, Bubble, Officer, Needle, Chimpanzee, Rabbit, Fork, Bird

Let's Practice

Match the sound.

Circle the objects that begin with or contain the sound as the given letters.

B    	violin, baboon, balloon, box
AI	beans, boat, rainbow, grass
J	jar of jellybeans, jellyfish, ink, juice
OA	frog, goalkeeper, bus, boat
IE	thief, cookie, bird, chilli
EE	seesaw, milk, tea, cheese